TEEN STRONG

Boosting Black Voices WITH

Marley Dias

by Heather DiLorenzo Williams

FAST READS

full tilt PRESS

For Lauren, who stood up for what she believed in with passion and strength.

Marley Dias
TEEN STRONG

Copyright © 2022
Published by Full Tilt Press
Written by TK
All rights reserved.

Full Tilt Press
42964 Osgood Road
Fremont, CA 94539
readfulltilt.com

Full Tilt Press publications may be purchased for educational, business, or sales promotional use.

Editorial Credits
Design and layout by Sara Radka
Edited by Meghan Gottschall

Image Credits
Getty Images: BET/Paras Griffin, 19, Dia Dipasupil, 12, 27 (top), Disney/Alberto E. Rodriguez, 21, Elsa, 24, Foundation for Letters/Gustavo Caballero, 6, Ivan-balvan, 29, Jeff J Mitchell, 17, JetBlue/Bob Levey, 20, Klaus Vedfelt, 11, Manny Carabel, 16 (bottom), Robin Marchant, 15, Shorty Awards/Noam Galai, cover, 1, Stephen Maturen, 25, Teen Vogue/Vivien Killilea, 14, The Foundation for Women/Astrid Stawiarz, 3, The Foundation for Women/Monica Schipper, 18, The New York Women's Foundation/Monica Schipper, 26 (bottom), Tory Burch Foundation/Monica Schipper, 27 (bottom); Newscom: KRT/Chuck Berman, 16 (top), Polaris/William Wade Jr, 7, Splash News/Jen Lowery, 10, Splash News/Photo Image Press, 4, WENN/DS7/Derrick Salters, 22, 23; Pixabay: GDJ, 9; Shutterstock: Dragana Gordic, 8, Franzi, background, wavebreakmedia, 26 (top); Wikimedia: Anders Hellberg, 13

ISBN: 978-1-62920-906-7 (library binding)
ISBN: 978-1-62920-910-4 (ePub)

CONTENTS

Introduction

In 2016, Marley attended Black Girls Rock, a yearly awards show honoring Black women in entertainment, music, and other fields.

Eleven-year-old Marley Dias loved to read. But she was tired of reading the same kinds of books. The characters looked nothing like her. She wanted to read books about Black women and girls. *Brown Girl Dreaming* by Jacqueline Woodson was one of her favorites.

Marley and her mom were having pancakes after school one day. She was telling her mom about *Brown Girl Dreaming*. They also talked about Marley's frustration with reading. Marley's mom asked, "If you could change one thing, what would it be?" Marley thought about her book problem.

Marley decided to find a solution. She knew she had three options. She could go to a bookstore to buy what she wanted. She could ask authors to write more books about Black girls. Or she could go on a mission to find books with Black female characters. Then she could share those books with other girls.

Marley chose the third option. That decision changed her life. It also changed the lives of countless girls. Each would benefit from Marley's passion.

Getting Started

Marley's parents, Scott and Janice Johnson Dias, have encouraged their daughter to take an interest in her community from an early age, and have supported her efforts to make it better.

Marley Dias was born on January 3, 2005, in Philadelphia, Pennsylvania. Her parents are Dr. Janice Johnson Dias and Scott Dias. Marley lives with them in New Jersey. She is an only child. Marley loves her dog, Philly. She is a fan of fashion. She likes trying out the latest styles and is not afraid to make a statement.

Marley grew up watching **activism** in action. Her mother was born and raised in rural Jamaica. She is the co-founder and president of a group. It is called the GrassROOTS Community Foundation. Dr. Dias has devoted her life to helping families in low-income areas. She also published a book in 2021 called *Parent Like It Matters: How to Raise Joyful, Change-Making Girls*. The book helps parents teach their daughters to use their interests to make the world a better place. It was no surprise to Marley's parents that she became interested in activism herself.

Janice Johnson Dias founded the GrassROOTS Community Foundation with her friend Tariq Trotter. Trotter, who is better known as Black Thought, is a member of the group the Roots.

Marley's parents named her after Bob Marley, the well-known reggae singer from Jamaica.

activism: working for political or social change

One example of social action is collecting food and clothing to donate to people in need.

Learning to Make a Difference

The GrassROOTS Community Foundation has many programs. Several teach young girls how to make a difference in their communities. Marley was in one of those programs. She learned the difference between "social justice" and "social action." Social justice is the idea that everyone deserves an equal chance for political, economic, and social rights.

But Marley says social action is different. It means "you find an issue in your community and you create an **initiative** to solve that issue or to help people," she told *Elle* magazine. Marley has seen social action firsthand. She was on a trip to Ghana with her mother. She volunteered at an African Health Now health fair. She also served at an orphanage's Christmas event.

JAMAICA

Jamaica is a small Caribbean island south of Florida. It is known for its rainforests and beautiful beaches. Jamaica is also the birthplace of reggae music and its creator, Bob Marley. The Dias family has ties to the country. Marley's mother grew up in the small village of Retreat in Jamaica. She later lived in Kingston, the capital.

initiative: a proposed solution to a problem or issue

Becoming Teen Strong

Marley's mom is one of her biggest inspirations. She and her mom attended *Variety* magazine's Power of Women Luncheon together in 2016.

Marley was able to choose what she read for most of elementary school. But in fifth grade, students were required to read certain books. *Where the Red Fern Grows* and *Shiloh* were two of them. These books were about "white boys and their dogs." Marley was disappointed. She wanted her fellow students to read about female characters from different **ethnic** backgrounds.

Marley complained to her mother. Her mom asked, "So what are you going to do about it?" Marley's first step was **launching** a club. She started it with her two best friends. The group is called BAM (after Briana, Amina, and Marley). The girls won a Disney Friends for Change grant in 2016. Marley also launched a book drive. She wanted to collect books to share with other girls.

Marley wanted girls of all ages to see their own stories in the books they read in class and checked out at the library.

Although people of color make up 37 percent of the US population, only around 15 percent of the 3,700 children's books published in 2019 were written by Black, Latino, or Native American authors.

ethnic: related to a group of people and their culture
launch: to start something new, such as a business, club, or project

Getting It Done

Marley collected 1,000 books. Each book's **protagonist** was a Black girl. She sent the books to her mother's former elementary school in Jamaica. The hashtag #1000BlackGirlBooks became a label for Marley's project. The project turned into a **movement**. Marley collected thousands of books. They were for schools in Jamaica and Ghana. She also collected books for schools in her local community. Marley did not pick her own school at first. "I realized that even in all-Black spaces like Jamaica . . . the **narratives** of white people are still being pushed on to people," she told the *Guardian*.

Marley was a keynote speaker at the 2017 Forbes Women's Summit, where she shared the stage with Kim Kardashian and Kerry Washington.

Marley organized a reading party at the White House. She also spoke at the White House's United State of Women event. Michelle Obama and Oprah Winfrey spoke too. In 2018, Marley became the youngest person ever included on the *Forbes* 30 Under 30 list. That same year, she was also named one of *Time* magazine's 25 most influential teenagers.

GRETA THUNBERG

Marley is one of many teenagers gaining attention for their activism. Greta Thunberg is a well-known climate change activist. She has traveled around the world speaking to government organizations in several countries about protecting Earth's resources. Kids like Greta and Marley have gotten a lot of attention for their fresh, honest approach to solving big problems.

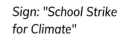
Sign: "School Strike for Climate"

protagonist: the main character in a story

movement: a campaign involving a group of people working together to solve an issue

narrative: a story that connects events or experiences in a way that supports a certain viewpoint

Inspiration

Marley's advice to other teens who want to solve problems in their communities is to use whatever they are most passionate and excited about as a starting point.

Marley saw that **systemic racism** was everywhere. It even showed up in books in classrooms and school libraries. Marley hoped her book drive could help change this. Many of the books on Marley's list include topics that are unique to Black girls. This includes natural hair. People who have natural hair do not use chemicals or tools to change the way their hair looks. Marley wants girls to have confidence. She does not want girls to feel like they have to look a certain way to be accepted.

Marley's book drive was inspired by Jacqueline Woodson's *Brown Girl Dreaming*. It is a novel about a young girl's experience with **segregation** and racism. Woodson was also inspired by Marley. She wrote an article about Marley in poetry for *Smithsonian Magazine*.

Author Jacqueline Woodson has written more than 35 books for children, teens, and adults. Woodson is known for tackling sensitive issues such as race, gender, poverty, and family.

Brown Girl Dreaming by Jacqueline Woodson is a novel written entirely in poetry.

---

systemic racism: discrimination against a group of people that is built into various parts of society, such as schools, politics, and the criminal justice system

segregation: separation of people because of their skin color

Making Connections

Natasha Anastasia Tarpley

Jacqueline Woodson is Marley's favorite author. But Marley was inspired by many other African American authors and artists. She is a fan of the children's book *I Love My Hair* by Natasha Anastasia Tarpley. The book celebrates hairstyles unique to Black girls. It promotes a positive self-image. Tomi Adeyemi is another of Marley's favorite authors. She wrote *Children of Blood and Bone*. Marley says she likes Adeyemi's books because there are not many Black people in fantasy and science fiction stories.

Tomi Adeyemi

Marley uses social media to inspire her many fans. She joined Instagram and Twitter in 2016 and Facebook in 2017. She speaks out on issues such as education, health, and race. Her followers include authors, actors, fellow activists, and her mom. Marley's posts promote things she loves, such as her hair, bright colors, funky glasses—and, of course, books and social action. Social media helps her connect with others and bring her passions to even more people.

BLACK LIVES MATTER

Marley uses her social media accounts to promote many other social action movements. One is Black Lives Matter (BLM). BLM began in 2013 after Trayvon Martin was shot and killed. The BLM movement is dedicated to using nonviolent protests to bring awareness to violent acts against Black people. In general, BLM encourages anti-racism and equity for Black people worldwide.

Work in Progress

Marley was a featured speaker at the Ms. Foundation's annual Gloria Awards in 2018. These awards honor people who are making a difference in the lives of women.

Marley has not slowed down since launching her #1000BlackGirlBooks book drive. Marley published her own book in 2018. It is called *Marley Dias Gets It Done: And So Can You!* The book is part **autobiography**, part activist handbook. It is filled with Marley's personal stories. There are tips for teens about how to change their communities. Booklists are also included.

Marley's advice to fellow teens is to find their passions. She told the *Guardian*, "If you're passionate about makeup, and you use that passion to highlight social issues, people will connect with your **authenticity**."

Director Ava DuVernay agrees with Marley. She was so impressed with her that she wrote the foreword for Marley's book. DuVernay directed Disney's 2018 film *A Wrinkle in Time*. The film has a Black lead actress. DuVernay became the first Black woman in history to direct a live-action film that earned $100 million at the box office.

Ava DuVernay is working to diversify the Hollywood film industry, much like Marley Dias is helping bring diversity to libraries and classrooms around the world.

Marley loves music almost as much as she loves books. Rapper Jay-Z is one of her favorite performers.

autobiography: a person's life story written by that person

authenticity: the state of being real or true to oneself

Branching Out

Marley and her mom launched Black Girl Book Club in 2017. The club is part of the GrassROOTS Community Foundation's summer camp series. The girls read books from Marley's #1000BlackGirlBooks list. They even got to meet Jacqueline Woodson. In 2019, Marley worked with JetBlue Airlines' Soar with Reading campaign. She helped the airline launch free book vending machines. The vending machines were filled with books for kids. Each has Black and brown main characters. Marley's book was one of them. Marley started a new #1000BlackGirlBooks collection drive in 2020. It is for schools in Ghana and Jamaica.

Since it launched in 2015, JetBlue's Soar with Reading program has placed book vending machines in cities across the United States, including New York City, San Francisco, California, and Houston, Texas.

In August 2020, Marley spoke at the **virtual** Democratic National Convention. She also produced and hosted her own TV show that year. The Netflix show is *Bookmarks: Celebrating Black Voices*. It features celebrities and artists. They read books about the experiences of Black people. One of the readers is Jacqueline Woodson.

A WRINKLE IN TIME

A *Wrinkle in Time* is based on a 1962 science fiction/fantasy novel. Director Ava DuVernay chose non-white actors to portray many of the story's main characters, who were white in the novel. Like Marley, she did not want to give the world another story told through the eyes of a white protagonist. DuVernay's cast included Storm Reid, Mindy Kaling, Oprah Winfrey, and Michael Peña.

virtual: an event or situation occurring not in person but with the help of technology

A Bright Future

Combining her passion for style and fashion with her desire to change the world, Marley spoke to a crowd at Macy's in New York City during Black History Month in 2020.

Marley loves curling up with a book in her room. But she also loves speaking to thousands of people from a stage. Reading was the bridge that led Marley to activism. Writing her own story opened the door to Marley's future.

In addition to her book, Marley also edited a special digital edition of *Elle* magazine. It is called "Marley Mag." She interviewed and wrote about Hillary Clinton and Ava DuVernay for the online magazine. She also modeled her favorite glasses and colorful lipstick in a photo shoot for "Marley Mag."

Marley plans to be a professional writer. She also hopes to be a magazine editor someday. But Marley doesn't want to write for just any magazine. She wants to start her own. She wants to continue promoting diversity, racial equity, and social action.

Marley was honored at the 2019 African American Literary Awards for the #1000BlackGirlBooks campaign.

Between 2016 and 2021, Marley's #1000BlackGirlBooks campaign collected more than 13,000 books.

In June 2020, Marley gave an emotional speech at a rally in her hometown following George Floyd's death. She stressed that young people must be active participants in the fight against racism.

teen strong

Marley is a voice of hope during a difficult time in the US. The COVID-19 crisis hit in early 2020. Stay-home orders put a stop to her library visits and public speaking. But Marley did not stop working. She read children's books out loud on Instagram. She also participated in many virtual events, such as the Rebel Girls Fest 2021. Throughout the fall of 2020 and spring of 2021, Marley chatted with former First Lady Michelle Obama, US Secretary of Transportation Pete Buttigieg, and former US Secretary of State Hillary Clinton about the need for more diversity in children's literature.

Marley Dias plans to be a part of that change. The teen hopes to someday host a summit for kids and teens. She wants to teach others how to launch their own social action projects. Marley also plans to keep reading and writing. Through her own words and the words of others, Marley has already started bringing about change. She is ready to lead her generation into a time when Black girl books are at the top of every required reading list.

THE PEN IS MIGHTIER THAN THE SWORD

Marley Dias believes that the underrepresentation of Black girls in young adult literature is a form of **covert** racism. She wants to combat racism by promoting books with Black protagonists. Marley was onto something. In 2020, George Floyd was killed during an arrest. Anti-racism protests were held around the world. Black community leaders and teachers began sharing booklists to help Americans learn about and fight against systemic racism.

George Floyd memorial in Minneapolis, Minnesota

....
covert: secret or hidden

Timeline

January 3, 2005

Marley Dias is born in Philadelphia, Pennsylvania.

November 2015

Marley decides to start a book drive to collect books with Black female protagonists. She launches #1000BlackGirlBooks.

2017

Marley is named *Success* magazine's 2017 Achiever of the Year.

2018

Marley publishes her book, *Marley Dias Gets It Done: And So Can You!*

2018

Marley is named to *Time* magazine's 25 Most Influential Teens list.

2018

Marley is named one of *Forbes* magazine's 30 Under 30. She is the youngest person ever to appear on this list.

2019

Marley becomes JetBlue Airlines' Soar with Reading ambassador.

2020

Marley re-launches #1000BlackGirlBooks on behalf of schools in Jamaica and Ghana, Africa.

2021

Marley appears on US Secretary of Transportation Pete Buttigieg's podcast, *The Deciding Decade*, to talk about the need for diverse representation in books, classrooms, and society in general.

QUIZ

#1
Who is Marley named after?

#2
What was Marley's book drive called?

#3
What was the name of Marley's social action club that she started with her best friends, Briana and Amina?

#4
Who wrote the foreword for Marley's book?

#5
What was Marley tired of reading about in fifth grade?

#6
Whose podcast did Marley appear on in 2021?

1. Bob Marley
2. #1000BlackGirlBooks
3. BAM (Briana, Amina, and Marley)
4. Movie producer Ava DuVernay
5. White boys and their dogs
6. Pete Buttigieg

ACTIVITY

Marley's advice to teens who want to make the world a better place is to find their passions and use them to connect with people. Marley's passion is books. What's yours? Figure out what your passion is and then come up with a way you can use that passion to help others.

MATERIALS

- computer with internet access
- notebook or journal

STEPS

1. Brainstorm your passions. Make a list of things you love, from favorite sports to music to hobbies. Circle a few that really inspire you.

2. Use the internet to research social action projects related to your circled items.

3. Next, brainstorm causes, issues, or problems that concern you. Choose one. An example might be an overcrowded animal shelter due to too many stray cats and dogs.

4. Finally, design a project based on one of the passions you picked in #1 that supports the issue you chose in #3. Love running? Plan a 5K to raise money for supplies to care for homeless pets. Crazy about baking? Host a bake sale fundraiser for your local animal shelter.

5. Share your plan with a teacher or coach and find out what your next steps are. Maybe you just thought of the next great social action project!

GLOSSARY

activism: working for political or social change

authenticity: the state of being real or true to oneself

autobiography: a person's life story written by that person

covert: secret or hidden

ethnic: related to a group of people and their culture

initiative: a proposed solution to a problem or issue

launch: to start something new, such as a business, club, or project

movement: a campaign involving a group of people working together to solve an issue

narrative: a story that connects events or experiences in a way that supports a certain viewpoint

protagonist: the main character in a story

segregation: separation of people because of their skin color

systemic racism: discrimination against a group of people that is built into various parts of society, such as schools, politics, and the criminal justice system

virtual: an event or situation occurring not in person but with the help of technology

READ MORE

Dias, Marley. *Marley Dias Gets It Done: And So Can You!* New York: Scholastic, 2018.

Rich, Kaelyn. *Girls Resist!: A Guide to Activism, Leadership, and Starting a Revolution.* Philadelphia: Quirk Books, 2018.

Weintraub, Aileen, and Laura K. Horton. *Never Too Young!: 50 Unstoppable Kids Who Made a Difference.* New York: Sterling, 2018.

Woodson, Jacqueline. *Brown Girl Dreaming.* New York: Penguin, 2014.

INTERNET SITES

https://grassrootscommunityfoundation.org
The official website for Dr. Janice Johnson Dias's foundation, which helps girls and women make lasting changes in their lives and greater communities.

https://marleydias.com/about/
Marley's website, which includes a bio and information about the #1000BlackGirlBooks campaigns.

https://www.oprahmag.com/entertainment/a33806475/netflix-bookmarks-show-books-host-celebrities/
Article containing information about Marley's Netflix show, including the show's trailer and guest readers, as well as details about Marley's book drives.

INDEX